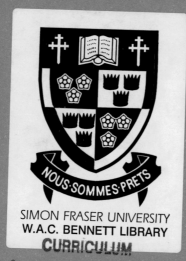

QUENNU
AND THE CAVE BEAR

A PREHISTORIC TALE BY
MARIE DAY

Owl

Owl Books are published by Greey de Pencier Books Inc.
179 John Street, Suite 500, Toronto, Ontario M5T 3G5

The Owl colophon is a trademark of Owl Children's Trust Inc.
Greey de Pencier Books Inc. is a licensed user of trademarks of Owl Children's Trust Inc.

Text and illustrations © 1999 Marie Day

Distributed in the United States by Firefly Books (U.S.) Inc.
230 Fifth Avenue, Suite 1607, New York, NY 10001

We acknowledge the generous support of the Canada Council for the Arts
and the Ontario Arts Council for our publishing program.

The author and publisher would like to thank Randall White, Professor in the Department of
Anthropology at New York University, for his generous assistance in the research for this book.

Cataloguing in Publication Data

Day, Marie
    Quennu and the cave bear

ISBN 1-895688-86-8 (bound) ISBN 1-895688-87-6 (pbk.)

I. Title.

PS8557.A94Q46 1999   jC813'.54   C98-932287-4
PZ7.D28Qu 1999

Design and art direction: Mary Opper

Printed in Hong Kong

A   B   C   D   E   F

DEDICATION

For Naomi, who we call Cuh, and Vanessa,
who we call Quennu

uennu was not afraid of very much. She had been taught to keep her distance from the fierce animals that shared the valley with her people. So she wasn't afraid of the woolly mammoths with their long tusks, or the jaws of the sabre-toothed tigers. She wasn't afraid of the owl's lonely call and the hyena's shrill laughter. She wasn't afraid when her brothers, Scarp and Willig, ran and hid, leaving her all alone.

Unlike most of the children, Quennu wasn't afraid of the Shaman. She was curious about the bundles of bones and plants he used to make magic for the people, and she wondered what he learned from watching signs in the sky. Quennu sat quietly near him as he watched the sun and moon move in their paths, and listened to the stories he told her again and again.

But Quennu was afraid of cave bears. She knew about the bears — huge creatures, two or three times the size of the biggest man among the people, with sharp teeth and tearing claws. When she listened to stories about the bears, she could almost see one looming in the shadows, its eyes gleaming at her.

One morning, Quennu climbed up to her favorite place, high on the hill. When she was far above the valley, she opened her hand to look at the special thing she held tight in her closed fist. It was the tooth of a bear. "You need a charm," the Shaman had said when he placed it in her palm, "to be safe from the bear." Quennu could feel the power sleeping inside it.

The tooth was hard and smooth and almost as long as Quennu's hand. She put it on a thong to wear around her neck. The charm felt solid and heavy where it was hanging against her skin.

From her perch on the hill, Quennu heard sharp bursts of sound, and recognized her mother's shrill flute calling her to come down.

There was much work to do. The people were all busy preparing lamps, weaving ropes, digging red and yellow earth from the hillside, making flutes from bird bones, and collecting moss and sticks. Quennu helped her mother pack colored clay into small hide bags. The Shaman would soon lead them to the place where they would all make magic.

The Shaman looked to the sky and, with a loud clap of his hands, let the people know it was time to set out. Everyone carried something — food, wood for the fire, animal hides, tools for painting. Quennu's parents joined the group, just behind the Shaman and the elders. Quennu trailed near the back with Scarp and Willig and the other children. She clutched her whistle made of a bird bone. Her brothers' flutes were made of eagle bones, carved and decorated by their father.

The people moved quickly down the familiar valley. The children ran around and played and explored, but there was always a grown-up watching to make sure they didn't stray too far from the rest of the clan. Once in a while, a whistle rang through the still air, calling a child who had straggled too far behind.

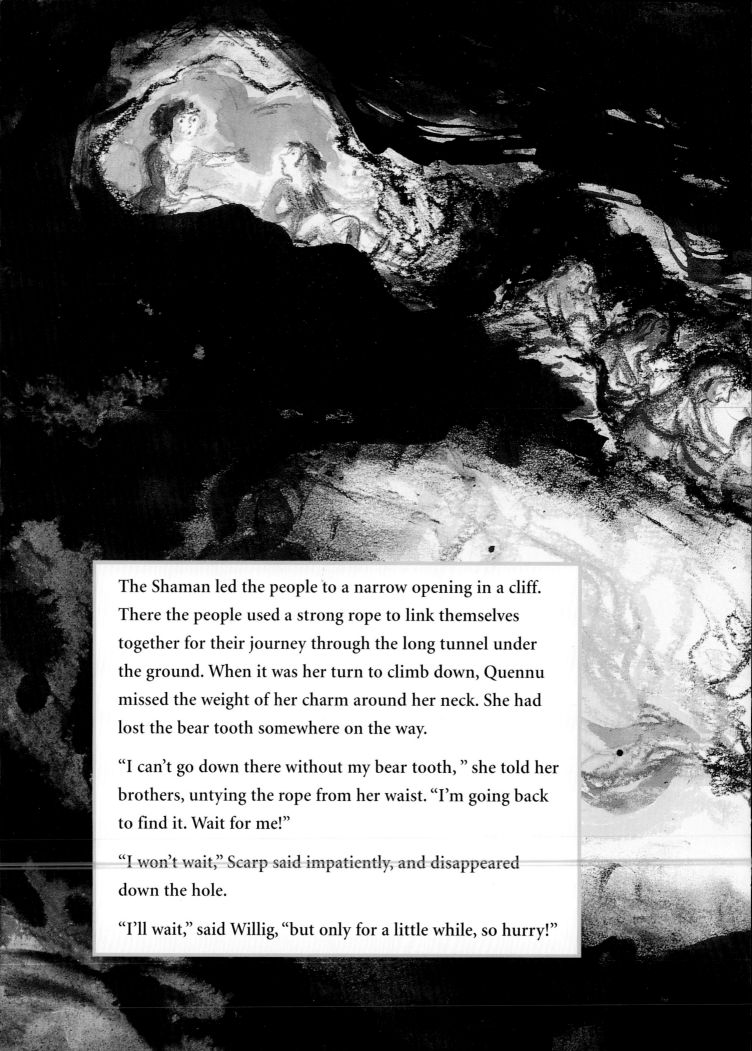

The Shaman led the people to a narrow opening in a cliff. There the people used a strong rope to link themselves together for their journey through the long tunnel under the ground. When it was her turn to climb down, Quennu missed the weight of her charm around her neck. She had lost the bear tooth somewhere on the way.

"I can't go down there without my bear tooth," she told her brothers, untying the rope from her waist. "I'm going back to find it. Wait for me!"

"I won't wait," Scarp said impatiently, and disappeared down the hole.

"I'll wait," said Willig, "but only for a little while, so hurry!"

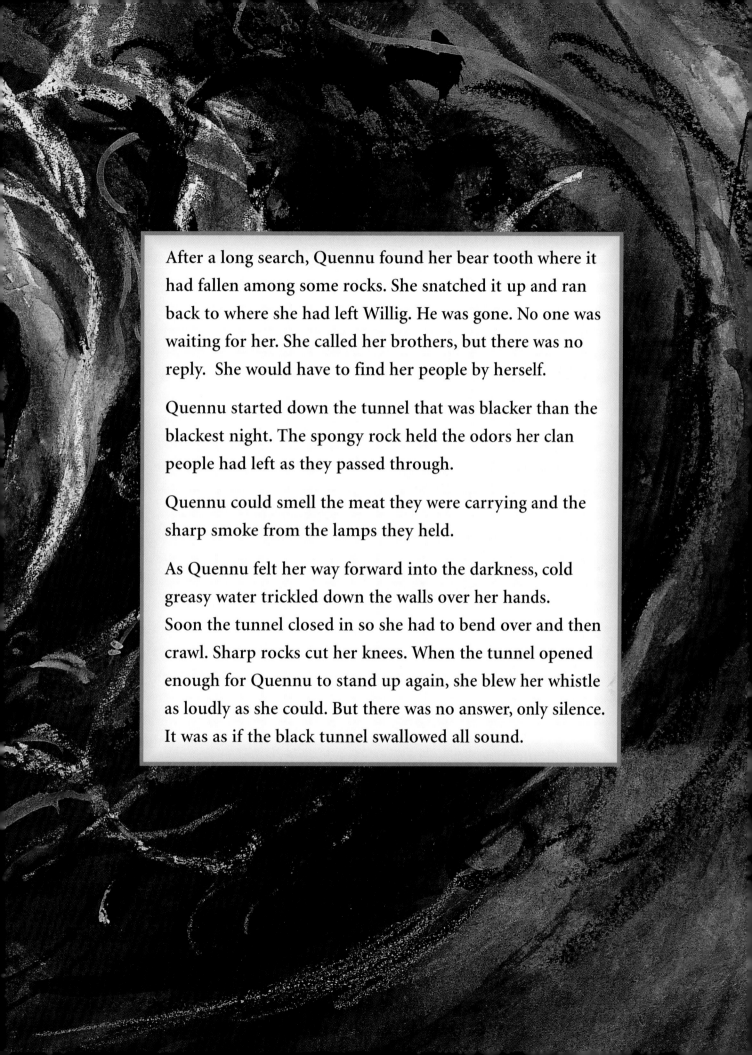

After a long search, Quennu found her bear tooth where it had fallen among some rocks. She snatched it up and ran back to where she had left Willig. He was gone. No one was waiting for her. She called her brothers, but there was no reply. She would have to find her people by herself.

Quennu started down the tunnel that was blacker than the blackest night. The spongy rock held the odors her clan people had left as they passed through.

Quennu could smell the meat they were carrying and the sharp smoke from the lamps they held.

As Quennu felt her way forward into the darkness, cold greasy water trickled down the walls over her hands. Soon the tunnel closed in so she had to bend over and then crawl. Sharp rocks cut her knees. When the tunnel opened enough for Quennu to stand up again, she blew her whistle as loudly as she could. But there was no answer, only silence. It was as if the black tunnel swallowed all sound.

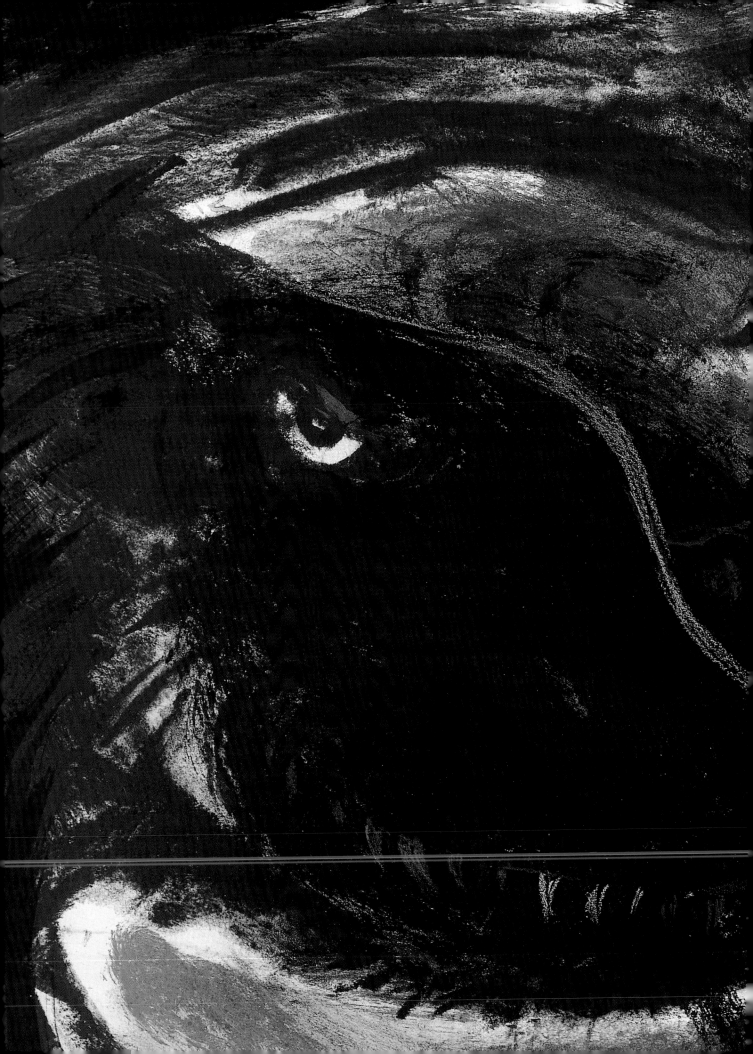

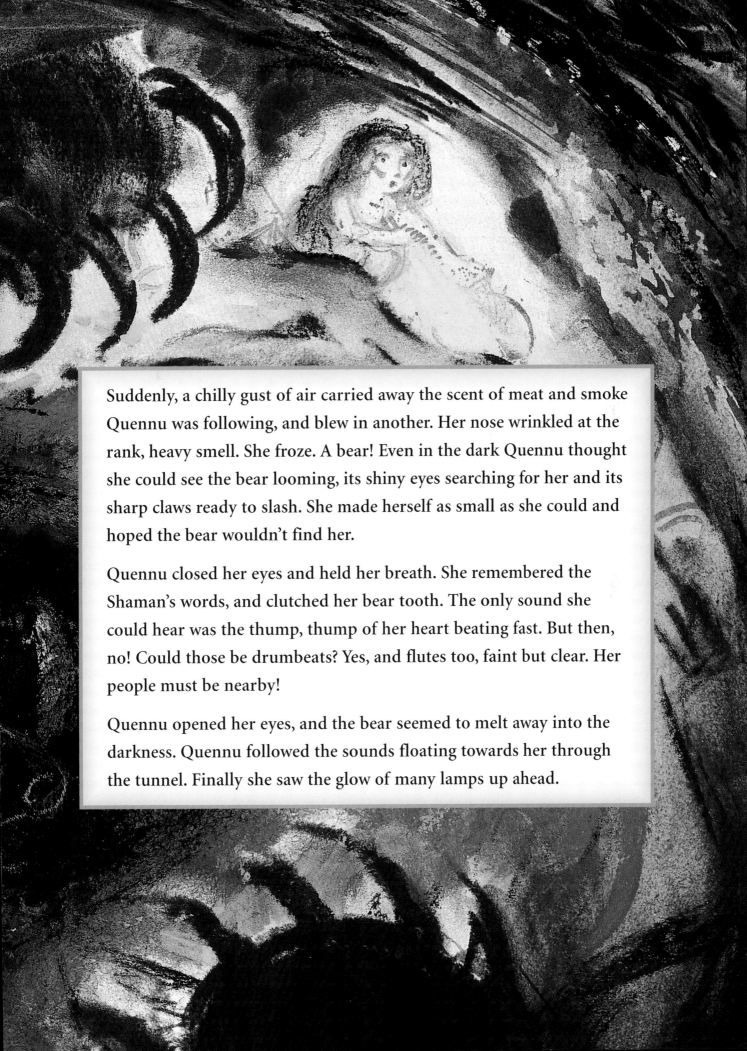

Suddenly, a chilly gust of air carried away the scent of meat and smoke Quennu was following, and blew in another. Her nose wrinkled at the rank, heavy smell. She froze. A bear! Even in the dark Quennu thought she could see the bear looming, its shiny eyes searching for her and its sharp claws ready to slash. She made herself as small as she could and hoped the bear wouldn't find her.

Quennu closed her eyes and held her breath. She remembered the Shaman's words, and clutched her bear tooth. The only sound she could hear was the thump, thump of her heart beating fast. But then, no! Could those be drumbeats? Yes, and flutes too, faint but clear. Her people must be nearby!

Quennu opened her eyes, and the bear seemed to melt away into the darkness. Quennu followed the sounds floating towards her through the tunnel. Finally she saw the glow of many lamps up ahead.

Quennu stumbled out of the dark tunnel and stared into the vast cavern full of firelight and movement. Stone icicles sparkled overhead, each with a diamond drop of water hanging from its tip. This was the place of magic.

The cavern was filled with the sounds of drums and the singing and chanting of the people. In the middle of the cave, the Shaman led dancers around the glowing light of lamps and torches. Quennu saw her father there, jumping and prancing. The dancers moved like all the different animals — horses and mammoths, reindeer and bison, even the flying birds.

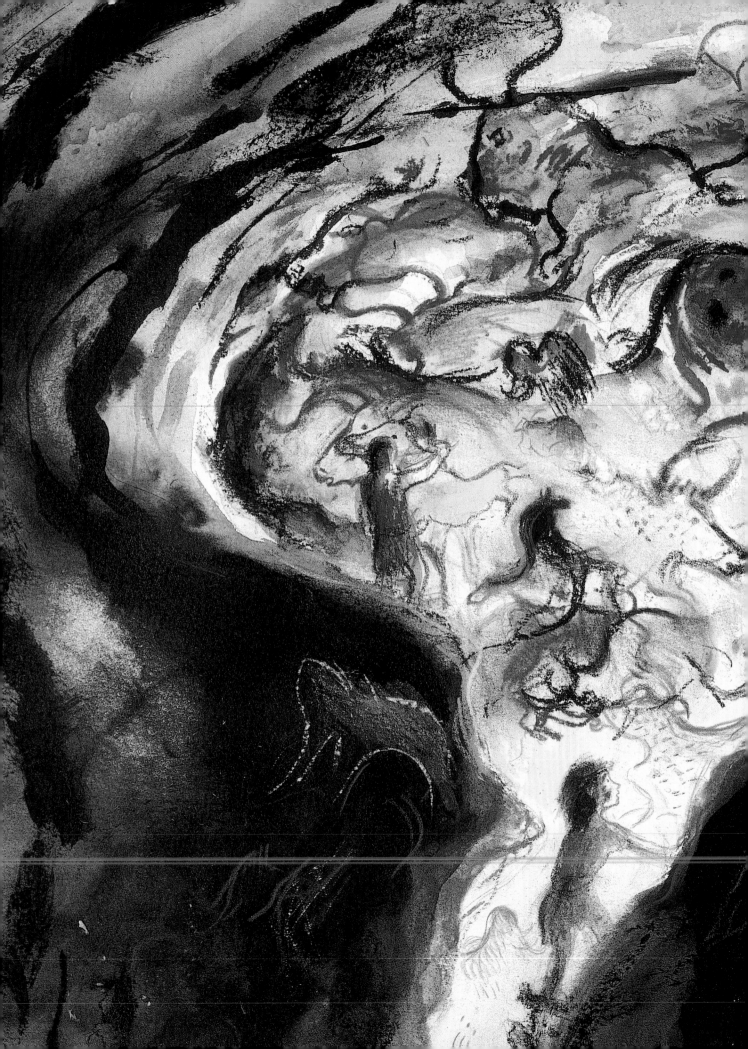

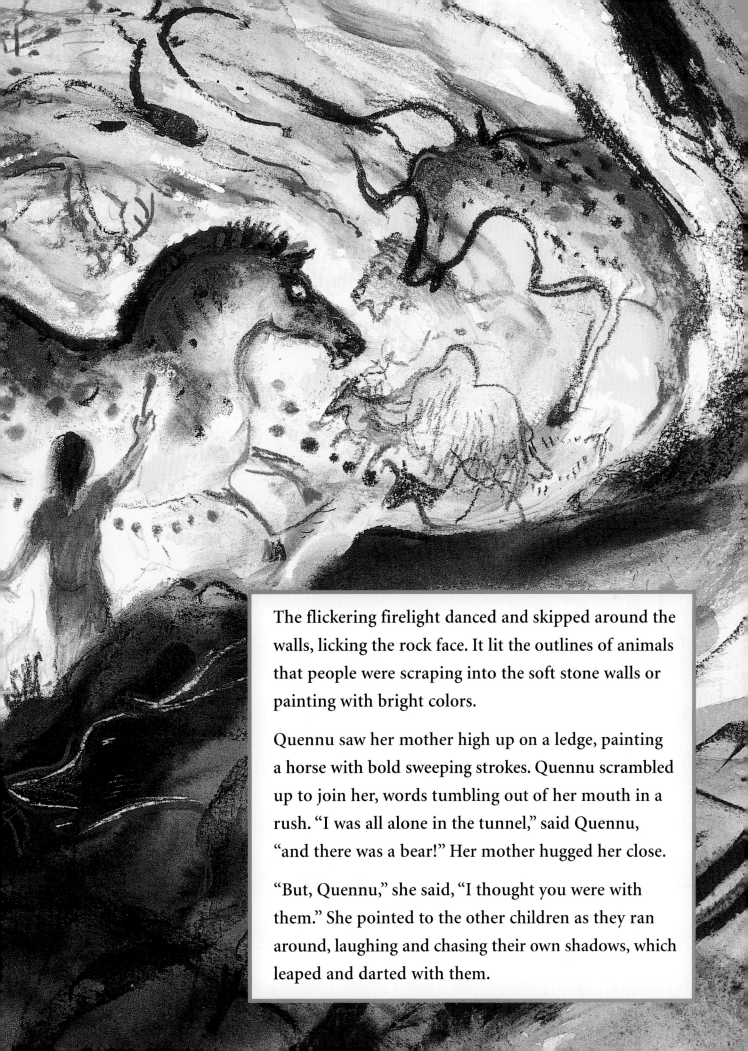

The flickering firelight danced and skipped around the walls, licking the rock face. It lit the outlines of animals that people were scraping into the soft stone walls or painting with bright colors.

Quennu saw her mother high up on a ledge, painting a horse with bold sweeping strokes. Quennu scrambled up to join her, words tumbling out of her mouth in a rush. "I was all alone in the tunnel," said Quennu, "and there was a bear!" Her mother hugged her close.

"But, Quennu," she said, "I thought you were with them." She pointed to the other children as they ran around, laughing and chasing their own shadows, which leaped and darted with them.

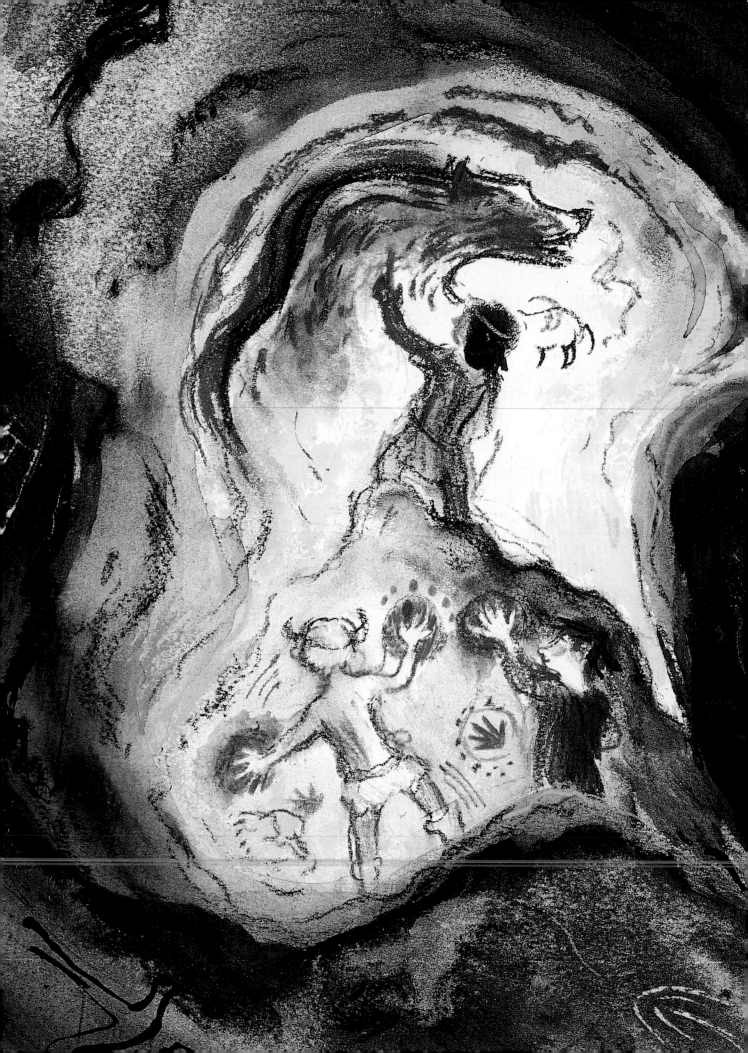

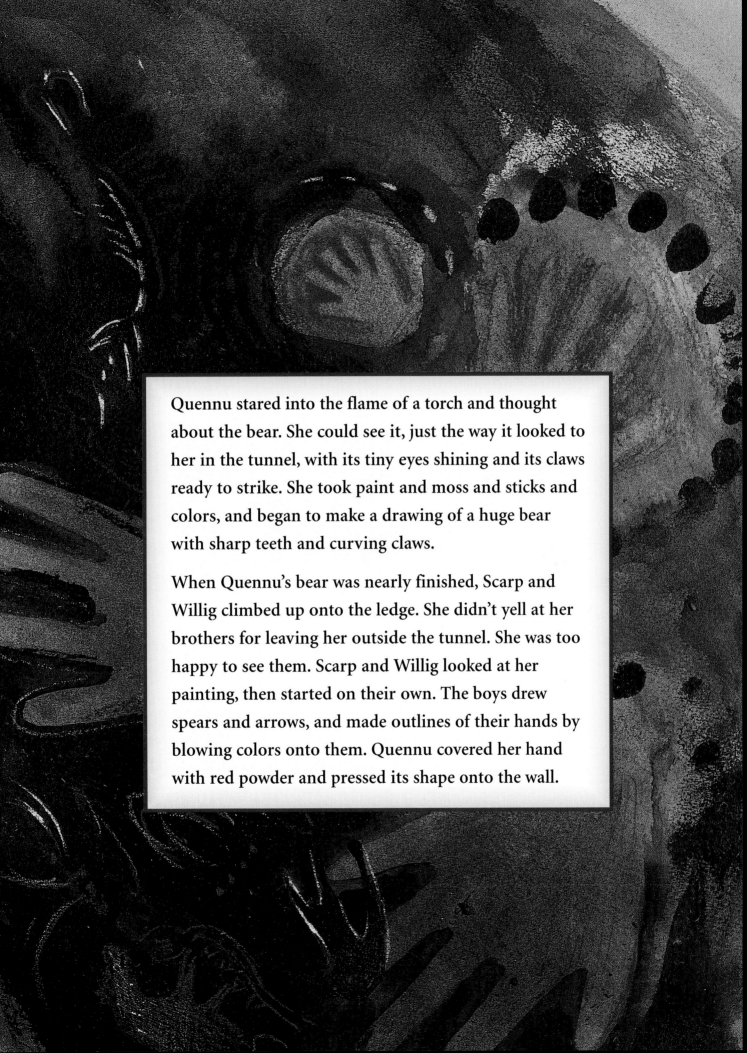

Quennu stared into the flame of a torch and thought about the bear. She could see it, just the way it looked to her in the tunnel, with its tiny eyes shining and its claws ready to strike. She took paint and moss and sticks and colors, and began to make a drawing of a huge bear with sharp teeth and curving claws.

When Quennu's bear was nearly finished, Scarp and Willig climbed up onto the ledge. She didn't yell at her brothers for leaving her outside the tunnel. She was too happy to see them. Scarp and Willig looked at her painting, then started on their own. The boys drew spears and arrows, and made outlines of their hands by blowing colors onto them. Quennu covered her hand with red powder and pressed its shape onto the wall.

Beat by beat, the drums started getting softer. One by one, the dancers began to drop to the ground, exhausted. The tired artists put down their tools and climbed down to join them. Soon, everyone was falling asleep and all was silent, except for the drip, drip of water falling from the tips of the stone icicles.

Quennu took one last look at her bear painting as she slid into sleep beside her mother. All around her were pictures of lions, panthers and hyenas, wild bulls and rhinos, and horses with black manes that streamed across the cavern walls like swirling stars. In the flickering light of the lamps, the painted creatures seemed alive. Quennu could almost hear their pawing and snorting, and the pounding of their hoofs as they galloped across the walls in the place of magic.

The bustle of a crowd close by woke Quennu out of a sound sleep. It was time for the clan to start the journey back through the passage that twisted through the blackness. Quennu felt safe with her people. She kept one hand on the rope joining her to her brothers, and the other on the charm hanging from her neck. Whenever they passed a place where the tunnel branched off, she wondered if the bear was lurking in the darkness.

One by one the people climbed out into the world of clear blue sky and sunshine. They blinked at the bright light, and drew in deep breaths of the fresh, clean air.

Back in the peaceful valley, the strange underground world seemed very far away. But Quennu would never forget the blackness of the tunnel and the wonder of the place of magic. As she ran through the long grass and on up the hill, the warm sun on her back felt better than it had ever felt before. The sight of her father and the other hunters gathering their spears and bows reminded Quennu of the animals running across the walls in the cave.

Alone in her favorite place with the valley spread out before her, Quennu thought about her adventure deep under the earth. She remembered how it felt to paint the bear on the cavern wall, and felt a rush of happiness. Far below, she caught sight of Scarp and Willig playing, following the hunters down the valley and pretending to join the hunt. Quennu jumped up and ran to go with them, her bear tooth bouncing on its leather thong.

A long, long time has passed since Quennu's people made their magic in the mysterious cave. In the cavern where drumbeats once echoed, the only sound is the drip, drip of water falling from the giant icicles of stone. All that is left of the lamps and torches that burned so bright are ashes and soot.

But in that place of magic deep inside the earth, great creatures still gallop across the hills and valleys of eternity. And somewhere in the darkness, Quennu's painted bear still waits, its fierce eyes gleaming.

THE FIRST ARTISTS

As long as 30,000 years ago, our ancestors painted beautiful pictures in caves deep inside the earth. They travelled to the caves through tunnels that followed steep climbs and sharp drops, and that were in places only high enough to crawl through. In the dark they kept contact with each other by holding on to ropes woven from plant fibres.

They made flutes from the bones of birds and used them to figure out the size of caves and caverns underground by sounding notes and listening carefully for echoes. People sent messages to each other with them as well.

In the caves, they made paintings of animals by the light of torches and lamps filled with animal fat. The artists applied the colors with moss or sticks or even their hands and fingers. Their paints were made from earth pigments and charcoal mixed with fat. We don't know how often people returned to the caves to make magic and paint on the walls. But even thousands of years after the first paintings were made, people were still travelling underground to add to them.

The paintings show that the artists were familiar with animals that no longer live in those parts of the world. In Europe, caves are painted with rhinoceroses, lions, and cave bears. Now extinct, these huge bears were one-and-a-half times the size of grizzly bears today.

All over the world, caves visited by ancient people have been, and continue to be, discovered. As scientists explore these places, they are very careful to preserve clues about how our ancestors lived. As recently as 1994, a cave full of images of animals — including a panther, an owl, and even a hyena — was found.